CONTENTS

Author's Preface

This is the music of the black men and women who entered the New World in chains, endured centuries of bondage, and emerged as African Americans, proud and free. In these slave songs, we hear the true voice of the pre–Civil War black South.

"Slave songs" is not a precise term. It refers to spirituals, work chants, hymns, ballads of sorrow, protest songs, and humorous ditties. It also includes songs *about* rather than *by* the enslaved Africans. Among them are "I Am Sold and Going to Georgia" and "Darling Nellie Gray," both written by white northern abolitionists and included in this collection.

Then there are the minstrel songs, such as "Jump Jim Crow" and "Ole Zip Coon." Featuring exaggerated southern black dialect, these white-authored works celebrate a world that never was: a sunny country populated by carefree "darkies" who spent their days singing and dancing. Minstrel songs were the hits of the 19th century.

"Ballad of Harriet Tubman" and "Follow the Drinking Gourd" belong to yet another category: modern white composers' songs about black people and their history. "Ballad" is the work of 20th-century troubadour Woody Guthrie; this version of "Follow the Drinking Gourd" was adapted by Lee Hays and the Weavers, folk-singing icons of the 1960s.

The words of these songs come from the people who created them. Some of the language may offend modern ears, but faced with a choice between "sanitizing" the lyrics and maintaining historical accuracy, the editor has chosen the latter. Anyone who is uncomfortable about certain words or phrases—and certainly, many of us may be—should feel free to do some discreet editing. As with all tradi--tional music, interpretation depends as much on the performer as on the song itself.

Most of the old songs in this collection were first printed by William Francis Allen, Charles Picard Ware, and Lucy McKim Garrison, editors of the monumental 1867 book *Slave Songs of the United States*. These collectors, who gathered their material during an 1861 visit to South Carolina's Sea Islands, might have been surprised to know that it would survive for well over a century. But it has. Most of us have heard "Nobody Knows the Trouble I See," "Many Thousand Gone," or "Michael, Row the Boat Ashore."

Whatever their original source, these songs connect the enslaved Africans of centuries past with today's black Americans. Thus, they represent a vital link of American history. On a less serious note, they are also great fun to sing. Enjoy them!

Jerry Silverman

The Contribution of Blacks to American Art and Culture

Kenneth B. Clark

Historical and contemporary social inequalities have obscured the major contribution of American blacks to American culture. The historical reality of slavery and the combined racial isolation, segregation, and sustained educational inferiority have had deleterious effects. As related pervasive social problems determine and influence the art that any group can not only experience, but also, ironically, the extent to which they can eventually contribute to the society as a whole, this tenet is even more visible when assessing the contributions made by African Americans.

All aspects of the arts have been pursued by black Americans, but music provides a special insight into the persistent and inescapable social forces to which black Americans have been subjected. One can speculate that in their preslavery patterns of life in Africa, blacks used rhythm, melody, and lyrics to hold on to reality, hope, and the acceptance of life. Later, in America, music helped blacks endure the cruelties of slavery. Spirituals and gospel music provided a medium for both communion and communication. As the black experience in America became more complex, so too did black music, which has grown and ramified, dramatically affecting the development of American music in general. The result is that today, more than ever before, black music provides a powerful lens through which we may view the history of black Americans in a new and revealing way.

Three generations of an enslaved family gather at their cabin on a Beaufort, South Carolina, plantation in 1862.

5

This spiritual is one of the best loved of all the slave songs. "Spirituals have been referred to as 'sorrow songs,' and in some respects they were," notes historian Lawrence W. Levine in his acclaimed 1977 book, *Black Culture and Black Consciousness*. "The slaves sang of 'rollin' thro' an unfriendly world' [and] of feeling like a 'motherless child.'. . . But these feelings were rarely pervasive or permanent; almost always they were overshadowed by a triumphant note of affirmation. Even so despairing a wail as 'Nobody Knows' could suddenly have its mood transformed by lines like: 'One morning I was a-walkin' down. . . . Saw some berries a-hangin' down. . . . Just as sweet as de honey in de comb.'"

NOBODY KNOWS THE TROUBLE I SEE

to chorus

I pick de berry and I suck de juice,
    O yes Lord!
Just as sweet as de honey in de comb.
    O yes Lord!   *Chorus*

Sometimes I'm up, sometimes I'm down,
    O yes Lord!
Sometimes I'm almost on de groun'.
    O yes Lord!   *Chorus*

What make de Satan hate me so?
    O yes Lord!
Because he got me once and he let me go.
    O yes Lord!   *Chorus*

Unlike "Nobody Knows the Trouble I See," this song—based on a phrase that has echoed through years of black American song—strikes a note of pure grief. A later blues composer, Richard M. Jones, attached an optimistic ending to his popular 1926 version of the song:

Trouble in mind, I'm blue,
But I won't be blue always,
For the sun will shine in my back door some-day.

I Am A-Trouble in the Mind

I am a-trou-ble in the mind, O, I am a-trou-ble in the mind.

I ask my Lord what shall I do,

I am a trou-ble in the mind. I'm a trou-ble in the mind, what you

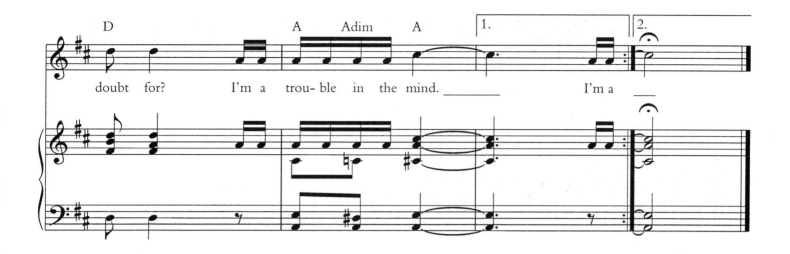

An elderly Alabaman, freed from slavery almost four decades earlier, picks out a tune on his banjo in 1902.

The narrative style and the melodic line of this 1856 song bear the unmistakable imprint of white hands: its composer was Benjamin R. Hanby, son of a white abolitionist minister from Ohio, and it caught on quickly among northern liberals. It was probably never sung by slaves themselves, but its catchy tune crossed the Atlantic Ocean to Scotland where, with a different set of lyrics, it is known as "Keep Your Feet Still, Geordie, Honey."

DARLING NELLIE GRAY

There's a low green _ val-ley by the old Ken-tuck-y shore, where we've whiled man-y

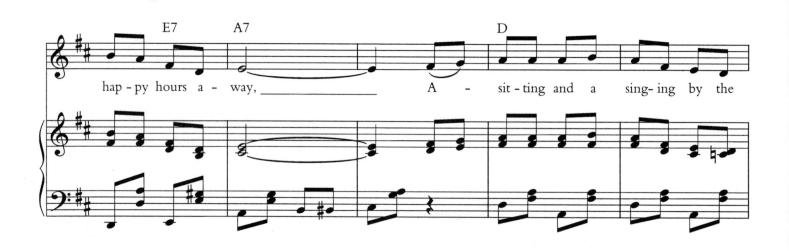

hap-py hours a-way, _____ A - sit-ting and a sing-ing by the

lit-tle cot-tage door, where _ lived my _ dar-ling Nel-lie Gray. _____

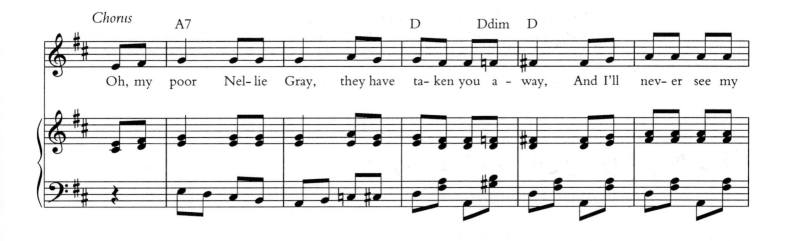

Chorus

Oh, my poor Nel-lie Gray, they have ta-ken you a-way, And I'll nev-er see my

dar-ling an-y-more. _____ I'm a - sit-ting by the riv-er and I'm

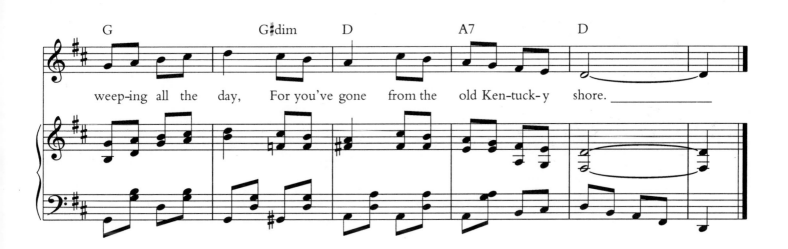

weep-ing all the day, For you've gone from the old Ken-tuck-y shore. _____

One night I went to see her but, "she's gone," the neighbors say.
The white man came and bound her with his chain.
They have taken her to Georgia for to wear her life away,
As she toils in the cotton and the cane. *Chorus*

The concept of not staying behind had a double meaning for the slave. In the purely religious sense, it referred to being saved and going to heaven. In the practical sense, it had a more immediate significance: escape to freedom. Hard experience had taught slaves to speak in roundabout ways, even in their songs. They chose their coded expressions carefully, exchanging encouragement and passing along information about uprisings or flights.

I Can't Stay Behind

I can't stay be-hind, my Lord, I can't stay be-hind. I hind.

Fine

There's room e-nough, room e-nough, room e-nough in the heav-en, my Lord.

Room e-nough, room e-nough, I can't stay be-hind.

to Chorus

I been all around, I been all around,
Been all around in the heaven, my Lord.
Been all around, been all around,
I can't stay behind. *Chorus*

I searched every room, searched every room,
Searched every room in the heaven, my Lord.
Searched every room, searched every room,
I can't stay behind. *Chorus*

The angels singin', the angels singin',
Angels singin' all around the throne.
Angels singin', angels singin',
I can't stay behind. *Chorus*

My father call, my father call,
My father call and I must go.
Father call, father call,
I can't stay behind. *Chorus*

Watched out of sight by his wife and daughter, a field hand departs for his day's labors in the Deep South.

The tune of "Go in the Wilderness" is the same as those of the black spiritual "The Old Gray Mare Came Tearin' Out of the Wilderness" and the familiar "The Old Gray Mare, She Ain't What She Used To Be." In the American presidential election of 1860, Abraham Lincoln's team borrowed the melody and imagery of these songs to create a campaign song:

> Old Abe Lincoln came out of the wilderness,
> Out of the wilderness, out of the wilderness,
> Old Abe Lincoln came out of the wilderness,
> Down in Illinois.

Singers often appropriate songs of other times and places, reshaping them to fit their own current needs. This is known as the folk process, and is perfectly exemplified by these "Old Gray Mare–Wilderness" songs.

GO IN THE WILDERNESS

go in the wil-der-ness, go in the wil-der-ness. Mourn-in', broth-er,

go in the wil-der-ness, I wait up-on the Lord.

to Chorus

If you want to be a Christian, go in the wilderness,
Go in the wilderness, go in the wilderness.
Mournin', brother, go in the wilderness,
I wait upon the Lord.   *Chorus*

similarly

You want to get religion . . .   *Chorus*

If you spec' to be connected . . .   *Chorus*

O weepin' Mary . . .   *Chorus*

'Flicted sister . . .   *Chorus*

Say, ain't you a member? . . .   *Chorus*

Half-done Christian . . .   *Chorus*

Come, backslider . . .   *Chorus*

Baptist member . . .   *Chorus*

Jesus a-waitin' to meet you in de wilderness . . .   *Chorus*

Like the Valiant Soldier, the angel Gabriel was an all-time favorite among America's enslaved blacks. Gabriel appears in both straightforward spirituals and secular (nonreligious) songs. Sometimes he shows up almost out of the blue, coming in at the end of a song that starts out in a completely nonreligious mood. This example of a surprise appearance by Gabriel was recorded in 1912 in Kentucky by white folklorist John Jacob Niles.

I got a yellow gal,
She is my honey,
She's a workin'-woman,
Gives me money.
Gabriel, Gabriel, oil you horn,
Get yourself ready for de Resurrection morn.
Great day comin'
Comin' soon.

BLOW YOUR TRUMPET, GABRIEL

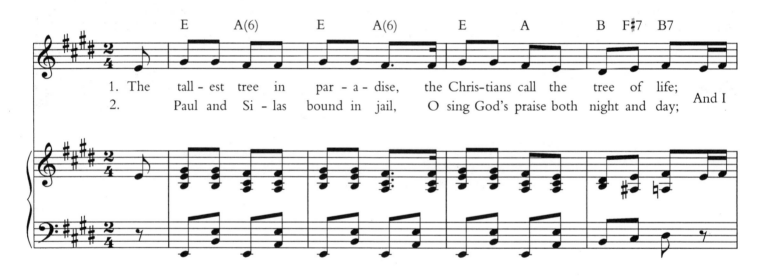

1. The tall-est tree in par-a-dise, the Chris-tians call the tree of life;
2. Paul and Si-las bound in jail, O sing God's praise both night and day; And I

hope that trump might blow me home to the new Je-ru-sa-lem.

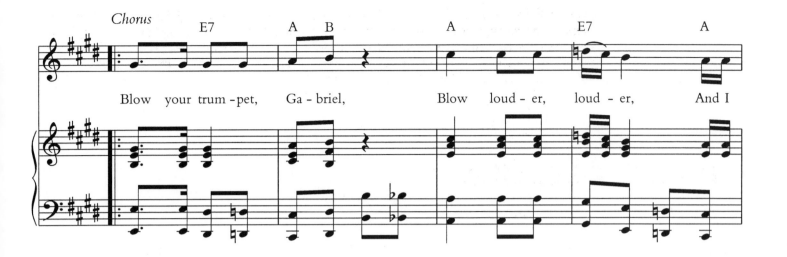

Blow your trum-pet, Ga-briel, Blow loud-er, loud-er, And I

hope that trump might blow me home to the new Je-ru - sa-lem.

The 1867 collection *Slave Songs of the United States* included this hymn. William Francis Allen, one of the book's editors, said that the words of "Praise, Member" came from the Bible and other Christian sources, but that the music was the slaves' own. Allen called such songs "the natural and original production of a race of remarkable musical capacity . . . retaining a distinct tinge of their native Africa." As it so often does in black religious music, the image of the Valiant Soldier appears in "Praise, Member" (a *member*, of course, is a fellow churchgoer).

PRAISE, MEMBER

want some val – iant sol – dier to help me bear the cross.

to Chorus

O soldier's is a good old fight,
And I hain't but one more river to cross.
I want some valiant soldier to help me bear the cross.

similarly

O I look to de East, and I look to de West . . .

O I wheel to de right, and I wheel to de left . . .

An extended southern family prepares for a Sunday afternoon of hymn singing.

Moses was the slaves' greatest hero. As one Union chaplain noted during a visit to Alabama in 1865, "Moses is their *ideal* of all that is high, and noble, and perfect, in man." The enslaved Africans never tired of recounting the triumphs of the "Hebrew chillen"; they sang that the "mighty rocky road" that they must travel was the same "rough, rocky road what Moses done travel."

Nowhere in the entire literature of slave spirituals is the identification between the black slave and the biblical Israelite more direct than in "Go Down, Moses." To complete the historical circle, today's Jews often sing this stirring slave song during the Passover *seder*, the meal that celebrates the Hebrews' escape from slavery in Egypt.

GO DOWN, MOSES

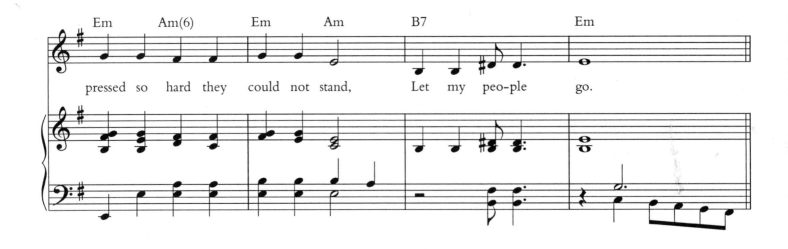

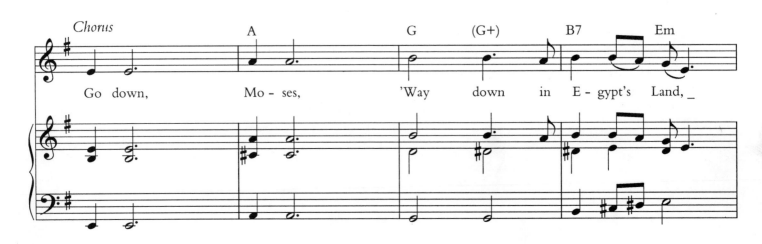

Tell ol' Phar - aoh, To let my peo-ple go.

Thus saith the Lord, bold Moses said,
Let my people go,
If not, I'll smite your first-born dead,
Let my people go.   *Chorus*

No more shall they in bondage toil,
Let them come out with Egypt's spoil.   *Chorus*

The Lord told Moses what to do,
To lead the Hebrew children through.   *Chorus*

O come along Moses, you'll not get lost,
Stretch out your rod and come across.   *Chorus*

As Israel stood by the waterside,
At God's command it did divide.   *Chorus*

When they reached the other shore,
They sang a song of triumph o'er.   *Chorus*

Pharaoh said he'd go across,
But Pharaoh and his host were lost.   *Chorus*

Jordan shall stand up like a wall,
And the walls of Jericho shall fall.   *Chorus*

Your foes shall not before you stand,
And you'll possess fair Canaan's Land.   *Chorus*

O let us all from bondage flee,
And let us all in Christ be free.   *Chorus*

We need not always weep and mourn,
And wear these slavery chains forlorn.   *Chorus*

As one former North Carolina slave put it after the Civil War: "The children of Israel was in bondage one time, and God sent Moses to 'liver them. Well, I s'pose that God sent Abe Lincoln to 'liver us." Lincoln, in turn, admired and respected many blacks, and he was especially fond of black music. In his 1954 book, *Songs Lincoln Loved*, author John Lair notes that when the young Illinois lawyer won his first case, he celebrated by going to a corn shucking. Lincoln enjoyed himself thoroughly, especially when two black musicians sang what would become one of his favorite songs: "Who Laid de Rail?"

WHO LAID DE RAIL?

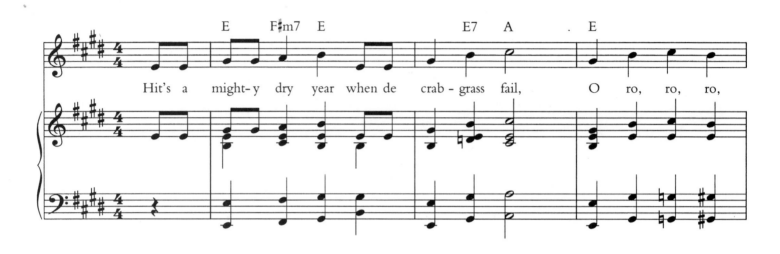

who laid de rail? Show me de nig-ger who laid de rail.

I'll hit him wid de hoe and I'll hit him wid de flail,
O, ro,ro,ro, who laid de rail?
I'll tro him thu de air like de buzzard do sail,
De big-foot nigger dat laid de rail. *Chorus*

Hit's might po' shuckin' when de red ear fail,
O, ro,ro,ro, who laid de rail?
De big-foot nigger dat kiss my gal
He hid dat red ear under de rail. *Chorus*

Before they could enter the Promised Land, the children of Israel had to cross the Jordan, a river that flows through scores of black songs. Slaves strongly identified with the plight and escape of the ancient Hebrews; to them, the connection between bondage in Egypt and in America seemed obvious. Abolitionist and former slave Frederick Douglass noted that when he and his fellow slaves sang about Canaan (the Promised Land), they had a special meaning. "'O Canaan, sweet Canaan/ I am bound for the land of Canaan,' symbolized something more than a hope of reaching heaven," said Douglass. "We meant to reach the *North*, and the North was our Canaan." Similarly, *wading in the water* and *crossing the Jordan* mean both going to heaven and striking out for freedom.

The melody of "Wade in the Water" is especially lyrical, and it lends itself to a rich harmonization.

WADE IN THE WATER

God's a - gon - na trou-ble the wa - ter.

It chills __ the bod - y, but
Tell all of my friends __ I'm

warms __ the soul, _____
com - ing too, _____

God's a - gon - na trou-ble the wa - ter.

to Chorus

Their meager belongings piled into a sagging wagon, members of a black southern family head north after the Civil War.

Printed before the Civil War, sheet music for "Jim Along Josey" shows a caricatured black man. The figure is wearing tattered clothes, missing one shoe, and grinning mindlessly as he performs an exaggerated dance step. This stereotyped happy, dancing slave never existed, of course. But that does not mean that the enslaved men and women from Africa did not enjoy their traditional dances.

In his 1966 book, *Before the Mayflower: A History of the Negro in America*, black scholar Lerone Bennett, Jr., writes, "Before the coming of the white man, music and rhythm were everyday things in Africa. . . . This attitude came to America. . . . In barns and open fields and in slave row shacks, slaves did jigs, shuffles, and 'set de flo.' They danced to the fiddle or the banjo and beat out rhythms with sticks and bones or by clapping their hands and stomping their feet."

JIM ALONG JOSEY

Hey get a-long, get a-long Jo-sey, Hey get a-long, Jim a-long Joe!

I'm de nigger that don't mind my troubles,
Because dey are noting more dan bubbles,
De ambition that dis nigger feels
Is showing de science of his heels.   *Chorus*

De fust President we eber had was Gen'ral Washington,
And de one we got now is Martin Van Buren,
But altho' Gen'ral Washington's dead
As long as de country stands his name shall float ahead.   *Chorus*

Oh! when I gets dat new coat which I expects to hab soon,
Likewise a new pair tight-kneed trousaloon,
Den I walks up and down Broadway wid my Susanna,
And de white folks will take me to be Santa Anna.   *Chorus*

My sister Rose de oder night did dream,
Dat she was floating up and down de stream,
And when she woke she begon to cry,
And de white cat picked out de black cat's eye.   *Chorus*

Now way down South not very far off,
A bullfrog died wid de whooping cough,
And de oder side of Mississippi as you must know,
Dare's where I was christen'd Jim along Joe.   *Chorus*

De New York niggers tink dey're fine,
Because dey drink de genuine,
De southern niggers dey lib on mush,
And when dey laugh dey say, "Oh Hush."   *Chorus*

Historians list a number of possible sources for the term *Jim Crow*. Many believe that the character was introduced by Thomas "Daddy" Rice, a celebrated white minstrel performer. Around 1830, Rice encountered Jim, a black slave who worked at Thomas Crowe's Livery Stable on Third Street in Louisville, Kentucky. A contemporary writer described Jim, who had earned local fame for his spirited dancing: "His left leg was stiff and crooked at the knee.... He was in the habit of crooning a queer old tune, to which he had applied words of his own. At the end of each verse he gave a peculiar step, 'rockin de heel'... and these were the words of his refrain: 'Weel about and turn about/ And do jist so/ Eb'ry time I weel about/ and jump Jim Crow.'"

First Rice, then other minstrel performers—including Micah Hawkins, who wrote this particular version of the song—adopted the "Jim Crow" song-and-dance routine, which became immensely popular with white audiences. But as the 19th century went on, *Jim Crow* came to be used in a new and ugly sense: it described the legal segregation of blacks and whites in almost all areas of American life, North as well as South.

JUMP JIM CROW

Come lis-ten all you gals and boys, I's jist from Tuck-y-hoe, I'm

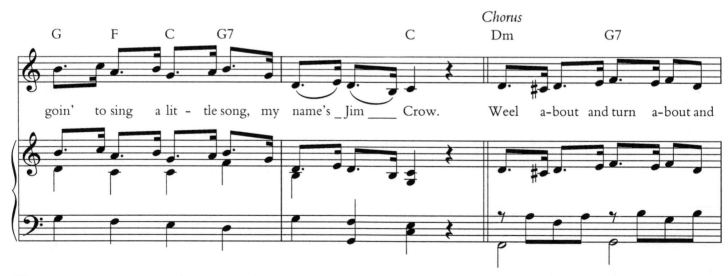

goin' to sing a lit-tle song, my name's Jim Crow. Weel a-bout and turn a-bout and

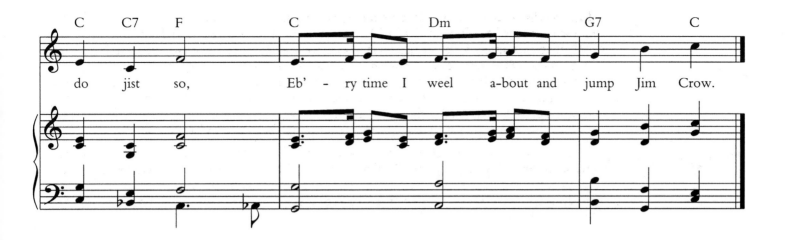

do jist so, Eb' - ry time I weel a-bout and jump Jim Crow.

Oh I'm a roarer on de fiddle,
And down in old Virginny,
They say I play de skyentific
Like Massa Pagannini.   *Chorus*

I went down to de riber,
I didn't mean to stay,
But dere I see so many gals,
I couldn't get away.   *Chorus*

I git 'pon a flat boat,
I catch de Uncle Sam,
Den I went to see de place
Wher dey kill'd Packenham.   *Chorus*

An den I go to Orleans
An feel so full of fight
Dey put me in de calaboose,
An keep me dere all night.   *Chorus*

When I got out I hit a man,
His name I now forget,
But dere was nothing left
'Cept a little grease spot.   *Chorus*

I wip my weight in wildcats
I eat an alligator,
And tear up more ground
Dan kiver 50 load of tater.   *Chorus*

I sit upon a hornet's nest,
I dance upon my head,
I tie a wiper round my neck
And den I goes to bed.   *Chorus*

Dere's possum up de gumtree,
An raccoon in de hollow,
Wake Snakes for June-bug's
Stole my half a dollar.   *Chorus*

A ring-tail'd monkey,
An a rib-nose baboon,
Went out de udder day
To spend de arternoon.   *Chorus*

Oh de way dey bake de hoe cake
In old Virginny neber tire,
Dey put de dough upon de foot,
An hole it to de fire.   *Chorus*

Oh by trade I am a carpenter,
But be it understood,
De way I get my liben is,
By sawing de tick oh wood.   *Chorus*

I'm a full blooded nigger,
Ob de real ole stock,
An wid my head and shoulder
I can split a horse block.   *Chorus*

According to author John Lair, "Nothing could more quickly rouse [Lincoln] from a fit of despondency than a rollicking song [such as] 'The Blue-Tail Fly,' which Lincoln called 'that buzzing song.'" The song is certainly amusing, but it also strikes a dark note. Like "Raise a Ruckus Tonight" (page 46) and many other slave songs, "Blue-Tail Fly" is a thinly disguised wish for a master's death.

THE BLUE-TAIL FLY

Slow - Recitative

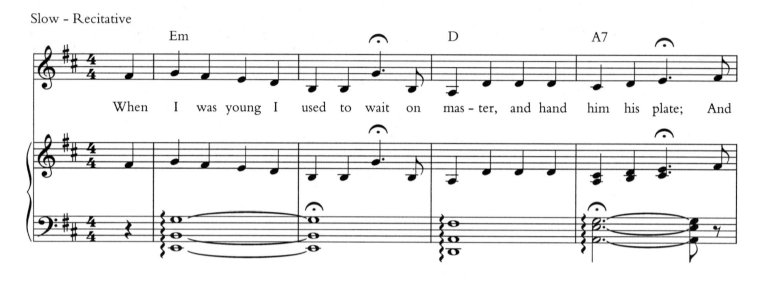

When I was young I used to wait on mas-ter, and hand him his plate; And

pass the bot-tle when he got dry, And brush a-way the blue-tail fly.

Jim-my crack corn, and I don'tcare, Jim-my crack corn and I don't care,

And when he'd ride in the afternoon,
I'd follow after with a hickory broom;
The pony being like to shy
When bitten by a blue-tail fly. *Chorus*

One day he ride around the farm,
The flies so numerous, they did swarm.
One chanced to bite him on the thigh;
The devil take the blue-tail fly! *Chorus*

The pony run, he jump, he pitch;
He threw my master in the ditch.
He died—and the jury wondered why—
The verdict was the blue-tail fly. *Chorus*

They laid him under a 'simmon tree;
His epitaph is there to see:
"Beneath this stone I'm forced to lie,
A victim of the blue-tail fly." *Chorus*

"Coon," a derogatory term applied to African Americans, may be a contraction of *raccoon*. The popular minstrel shows of the 19th century, which almost always featured white performers wearing "blackface" (burnt cork), were sometimes called *coon shows*. One pair of genuine black performers, the successful comedy team of Bert Williams and George Walker, billed themselves as "Two Real Coons" to set themselves apart from their blackface counterparts. The tune of "Ole Zip Coon," believed to have been written by Micah Hawkins in 1834, is probably better known as "Turkey in the Straw."

OLE ZIP COON

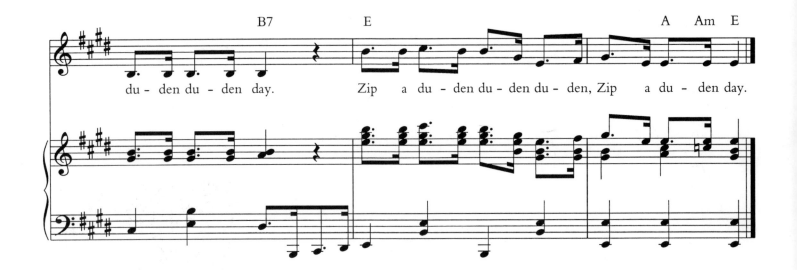

du – den du – den day.   Zip   a – du – den du – den du – den, Zip   a – du – den day.

O its old Suky blue skin, she is in lub wid me
I went the udder arternoon to take a dish ob tea;
What do you tink now, Suky hab for supper,
Why chicken foot an possum heel, widout any butter. *Chorus*

Did you eber see the wild goose, sailing on de ocean,
O de wild goose motion is a berry pretty notion;
Eb'ry time de wild goose, beckens to de swaller,
You hear him google google google google gollar. *Chorus*

I went down to Sandy Hollar t'other arternoon
And the first man I chanc'd to meet war ole Zip Coon;
Ole Zip Coon he is a natty scholar,
For he plays upon de banjo "Cooney in de hollar." *Chorus*

My ole Missus she's mad wid me,
Kase I wouldn't go wid her into Tennessee,
Massa build him barn and put in de fodder
Twas dis ting and dat ting one ting or de oder. *Chorus*

I 'pose you heard ob de battle New Orleans,
Whar ole Gineral Jackson gib de British beans;
Dere de Yankee boys do de job so slick
For dey cotch old Packenham an row'd him up de creek. *Chorus*

I hab many tings to tork about but don't know wich cum first,
So here de tost to ole Zip Coon before he 'gin to rust;
May he hab de pretty girls, like de King ob ole,
To sing dis song so many times, fore he turn to mole. *Chorus*

Cradling a live turkey, a southern food vendor waits for customers and enjoys her grandson's guitar playing.

Born in 1777, Kentuckian Henry Clay served as a U.S. senator, congressman, speaker of the House, and secretary of state. The politician, who called slavery "the deepest stain on the character of the country," also said he would "rather be right than be president," although he made three unsuccessful tries for the White House. Henry Clay's almost half-century in the political limelight made his name a household word, even landing it in such unexpected places as "Heave Away," this raucous black stevedore's song.

HEAVE AWAY

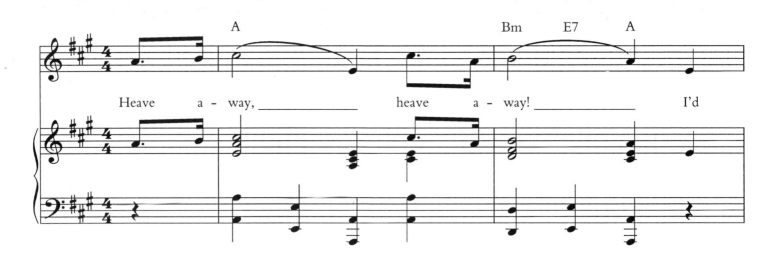

Heave a-way, _____ heave a-way! _____ I'd

rath-er court a yel-low gal than work for Hen-ry Clay, Heave a-way, _____ heave a-

way! _____ Yel-low gal, I want to go, I'd rath-er court a yel-low gal than

work for Hen - ry Clay. Heave a - way! _____ Yel- low gal, I want to go!

A farmer, part of black America's first freeborn generation, prepares to serenade his girlfriend .

A slave woman is singing a soft lullaby, full of sweet promises, to her mistress's child. The song is gentle and loving, but it has a bittersweet edge: as the woman croons to the white baby, her heart is with her own "poor little lambie," the neglected black baby who lies alone "way down yonder in the meadow."

ALL THE PRETTY LITTLE HORSES

Hush - a - bye, don't you cry, Go to sleep-y lit-tle ba - by.
When you wake you shall have All the pret-ty lit-tle

hor - ses. Blacks and bays, dap-ples and grays. Coach and four a- lit-tle

hor - ses. Hush a - bye, don't you cry, Go to sleep-y lit-tle ba - by.

Hush-a-bye, don't you cry,
Go to sleepy, little baby.
Way down yonder in the meadow,
Lies a poor little lambie.

The bees and the butterflies pecking out its eyes,
The poor little thing cried, "Mammy."
Hush-a-bye, don't you cry,
Go to sleepy, little baby.

Their own masters at last, newly emancipated Arkansas cotton farmers display the tools of their trade.

In his 1867 *Slave Songs of the United States*, William Allen noted that as slave oarsmen rowed their vessels across fast-flowing rivers, their leaders would keep them in time with such songs as this one. "Two measures are to be sung at each stroke," explained Allen, "the first measure being accented by the beginning of the stroke, the second by the rattle of the oars in the row-locks. . . . 'Michael row' [was] used when the load was heavy or the tide was against us."

MICHAEL, ROW THE BOAT ASHORE

Mi-chael, row de boat a-shore, hal-le-lu - jah. Mi-chael, row de boat a-shore, hal - le-lu - jah.

Michael boat a Gospel boat . . .

I wonder where my mudder gone . . .

See my mudder on de rock gwine home . . .

On de rock gwine home in Jesus' home . . .

Michael boat a music boat . . .

Gabriel blow de trumpet horn . . .

O you mind your boastin' talk . . .

Boastin' talk will sink your soul . . .

Brudder, lend a helpin' hand . . .

Sister, help for trim dat boat . . .

Jordan stream is wide and deep . . .

Jesus stand on t' oder side . . .

I wonder if my massa deh . . .

My fader gone to unknown land . . .

O de Lord he plant his garden deh . . .

He raise de fruit for you to eat . . .

He dat eat shall neber die . . .

When de riber overflow . . .

O poor sinner, how you land? . . .

Riber run and darkness comin' . . .

Sinner run to save your soul . . .

The thought of being "sold South" sent a chill of fear through every slave in the border states. Wretched as they were already, these people knew their lives would be infinitely worse if their masters sold them to a cotton or rice plantation in the Deep South. The theme naturally surfaces in many songs from the days of slavery. This one, with its rather flowery literary tone, is probably of white origin; others are unquestionably the work of black men and women. In 1857, for example, author John Dixon Long heard Maryland slaves singing this version of the song:

> *William Rino sold Henry Silvers;*
> *Hilo! Hilo!*
> *Sold him to de Georgy trader;*
> *Hilo! Hilo!*
>
> *His wife she cried, and children bawled,*
> *Hilo! Hilo!*
> *Sold him to de Georgy trader;*
> *Hilo! Hilo!*

Poet William Cullen Bryant encountered yet another version in 1843, when he heard a crew of South Carolina field hands singing what he called "this wild and plaintive air":

> *De speculator bought me.*
> *Oh hollow!*
> *I'm sold for silver dollars.*
> *Oh hollow!*
>
> *Boys, go catch the pony.*
> *Oh hollow!*
> *Bring him round the corner.*
> *Oh hollow!*
>
> *I'm goin' away to Georgia.*
> *Oh hollow!*
> *Boys, good-by forever!*
> *Oh hollow!*

I Am Sold and Going to Georgia

O! When shall we poor souls be free? When shall these slave-'ry chains be broke?

I am sold and going to Geor-gia, Will you go a-long with

me? I am sold and going to Geor-gia, Go sound the ju - bi -

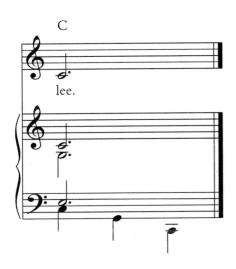

lee.

I left my wife and child behind,
They'll never see my face again. *Chorus*

I am bound to yonder great rice swamp,
Where my poor bones will find a grave. *Chorus*

Farewell, my friends, I leave you all,
I am sold, but I have done no fault. *Chorus*

Both during and after slavery, many black dance steps took their names from animals or animal movements; there have been the foxtrot, the turkey trot, and, as in "Charleston Gals," the pigeonwing. Former slaves' recollections of plantation days abound with references to dance. Louise Jones, for example, an elderly woman who had been a slave in Virginia, said in the 1930s that she clearly remembered "de music, de fiddles an' de banjos, de Jews harp, an' all dem other things. Sech dancin' you never did see befo'. Slaves would set de flo' in turns, an' do de cakewalk mos' all night." Blacks picked up certain European instruments, such as the guitar and the violin, from whites. But most of their instruments—the banjo, the musical bow, and a variety of stringed and percussive instruments—came with them from Africa.

CHARLESTON GALS

If he dies, we'll tan his skin, And if he lives we'll ride him a-gin.

Hi, ho, for Charles-ton gals! Charles-ton gals are the gals for me.

As I went a-walking down the street,
Up steps Charleston gals to take a walk with me.
I kep' a-walking and they kep' a-talking,
I danced with a gal with a hole in her stocking.   *Chorus*

A cook and her helper proudly display the makings of a favorite southern dish: green turtle soup.

"The Blue-Tail Fly" expresses the slaves' hostility rather subtly; "Raise a Ruckus Tonight" shows it openly. Like much grim slave humor—"laughin' to keep from cryin'," as the old saying put it— these songs often concerned a master or mistress who broke a promise of eventual freedom for a slave. Another version of "Ruckus," this one originating in Louisiana, contains these lyrics:

My ole mistress promised me
Before she died she would set me free.
Now she's dead and gone to hell,
I hope the devil will burn her well.

RAISE A RUCKUS TONIGHT

My old mistress promised me, raise a ruckus tonight,
"Sara, I'm gonna set you free," raise a ruckus tonight,
She lived till her head got slick and bald, raise a ruckus tonight,
And the Lord couldn't kill her with a big green maul, raise a ruckus tonight. *Chorus*

Yes, they both done promised me, raise a ruckus tonight,
But their papers didn't set me free, raise a ruckus tonight,
A dose of pizin helped them along, raise a ruckus tonight,
May the devil preach their funeral song, raise a ruckus tonight. *Chorus*

Born in 1800, Nat Turner grew up as a slave in Virginia's Southampton County. He had always been mystically inclined as well as deeply religious, and he developed a strong feeling that God had a special mission for him. Finally deciding that he was destined to lead his people out of bondage, Turner rounded up a group of supporters and, in 1831, led a bloody revolt. After slaughtering at least 57 white men, women, and children, Turner and his rebels fell to a huge force of white soldiers, planters, and militiamen. Turner was tried, convicted, and hanged, but news of his rebellion swept slave quarters throughout the South. "You can't keep the world from moving around," the slaves now sang, reassured that Turner's action had made freedom someday inevitable.

NAT TURNER

Words: traditional
Music by Jerry Silverman

You mought be reader and writer too,
And wiser than old Solomon the Jew;
But you can't keep the world from moving around,
And Nat Turner from the gaining ground.

And your name it mought be Caesar sure,
And got you cannon can shoot a mile or more;
But you can't keep the world from moving around,
And Nat Turner from the gaining ground.

*Ragged but beaming, this banjo player seems to express the post–Civil War mood of
black America.*

Henry Brown, born into slavery on a plantation near Richmond, Virginia, decided to escape in 1848. Samuel A. Smith, a white southerner who hated slavery and liked Brown, agreed to help. In 1848, Smith nailed his friend into a wooden crate, marked it "This Side Up," and shipped it to the office of an abolitionist society in Philadelphia. Emerging bruised but intact after his harrowing journey, Brown proceeded to sing "I waited patiently for the Lord, and He heard my prayer." Smith cheerfully served a jail term for his part in the escape, and for the next several years, Henry "Box" Brown toured northern cities, regaling large audiences with the improbable tale of his dramatic flight to freedom.

ESCAPE FROM SLAVERY OF HENRY BOX BROWN

Here you see a man by the name of Hen - ry Brown, Ran a-

way from the South to a north-ern town; which he would-n't have done but they caused him great pain, But they'll

nev - er do the like a - gain. Brown laid down the sho - vel and the hoe, ___

Down in the big box he did go;___ No more slave work for Hen-ry Box Brown, In the

box by ex - press to Phil - a - del - phi - a town.___

The orders they were given and the cars they did start,
Roll along, roll along, roll along.
Down to the landing where the steamboat met,
To bear the baggage off to the North. *Chorus*

When they packed the baggage on they turned him on his head,
There poor Brown liked to have died;
There were passengers on board who wished to set down,
And they turned the box on its side. *Chorus*

When they got to the cars they throwed the box off,
And down upon his head he did fall,
Then he heard his neck crack, and he thought he was dead,
But they never throwed him off any more. *Chorus*

When he got to Philadelphia they said he was in port,
And Brown he began to feel glad,
And he was taken on the wagon and carried to the place,
And left "this side up with care." *Chorus*

The friends gathered 'round and asked if all was right,
As down on the box they did rap,
Brown answered them saying "yes, all is right,"
And he was then set free from his pain. *Chorus*

Harriet Tubman was born a slave about 1821 in Dorchester County, Maryland. After escaping to the North in 1849, she made 19 secret and highly dangerous trips back to the South, each time escorting more blacks to freedom. Like many other Americans, folksinger Woody Guthrie found Tubman's story inspiring, and in 1944, he honored her by writing this ballad.

Nine years later, on the 40th anniversary of her death, Guthrie wrote Tubman a "letter." "I hope that I can do some little kind of a job or two of work everyday to hold on to all of your good things," he said in part. "More than a good 99 percent of everybody I know feel just the very same way that I feel about going right on and working and fighting till we kill that old snake of slavery that you . . . crippled as bad as you've crippled it."

Harriet Tubman's Ballad

Words by Woody Guthrie
Music: Traditional

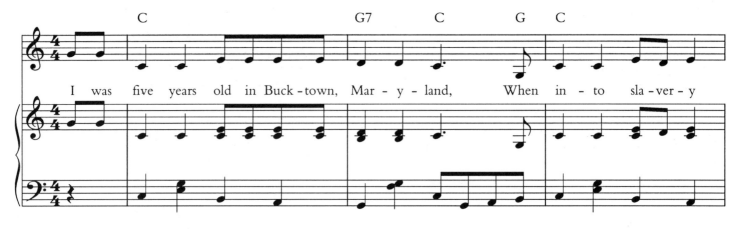

I was five years old in Buck-town, Mar-y-land, When in-to sla-ver-y

I was sent; I'll tell you of the beat-ings and of the fight-ing

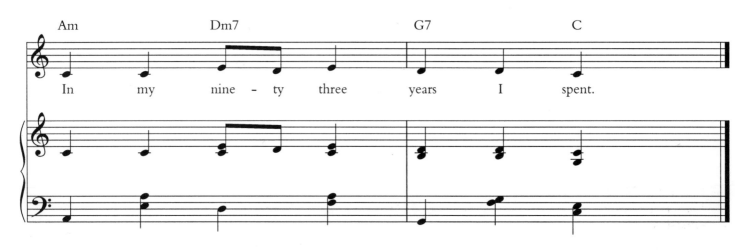

In my nine-ty three years I spent.

I helped a field hand make a run for freedom
When my fifteenth year was rolling around.
The guard, he caught him in a little store
In a little slavery village town.

The boss made a grab to catch the field hand,
I jumped in and blocked the door.
The boss then hit me with an iron scale,
And I went black down on the floor.

On a bundle of rags in our log cabin
My mother, she ministered to my needs.
It was here I swore I'd give my life blood
Just to fight to turn my people free.

In forty-four I married John Tubman,
I loved him well till forty-nine.
But he would not come and fight beside me,
So I left him there behind.

I left Bucktown with my two brothers,
But they got scared and went back home.
I followed my northern star of freedom
And I walked in the grass and trees alone.

I slept in a barn loft and in a haystack,
I stayed with my people in slavery's shacks.
They said I'd die by the boss man's bullets,
But I told them, "I can't turn back."

The sun was shining in the early morning,
When I finally come to my free-state line.
I pinched myself to see if I was dreaming,
I just could not believe my eyes.

I went back home and got my parents,
I loaded them into a buckboard hack.
We crossed six states and other slaves followed,
And up to Canada we made our tracks.

One slave got scared and tried to turn backward,
And I pulled my pistol in front of his eyes.
I said, "Get up and walk to freedom,
Or by this fireball you will die."

When John Brown hit them at Harper's Ferry,
My men were fighting right at his side.
When John Brown swung upon his gallows,
It was then I hung my head and cried.

"Give the black man guns and powder,"
To Abe Lincoln, this I said.
"You've just crippled the snake of slavery,
We've got to fight to kill it dead!"

When we faced the guns of lightning
And the thunders broke our sleep,
After we faced the bloody rainstorms,
It was dead men that we reaped.

Yes, we faced the zigzag lightning,
But it was worth the price we paid.
When our thunder rumbled over,
We'd laid slavery in its grave.

Come and stand around my deathbed,
I will sing some spirit songs.
I'm on my way to my greater Union,
Now my ninety-three years are gone.

HARRIET TUBMAN'S BALLAD

Words and music by Woody Guthrie. TRO—© 1972 Ludlow Music, Inc., N.Y. Used
by permission.

Escaping slaves traveled by the Underground Railroad—not an actual track, but a network of farmhouses or other buildings owned by militant abolitionists. At great personal risk, these anti-slavery activists fed, clothed, and lodged runaway blacks before sending them along to the next "station" on the "railroad." To get from one stop to the next, the fugitives "followed the drinking gourd," keeping their eye on the Big Dipper and its handle, which pointed toward the North Star and freedom.

FOLLOW THE DRINKING GOURD

Words and music adapted and arranged by Lee Hays
and the Weavers from a traditional song

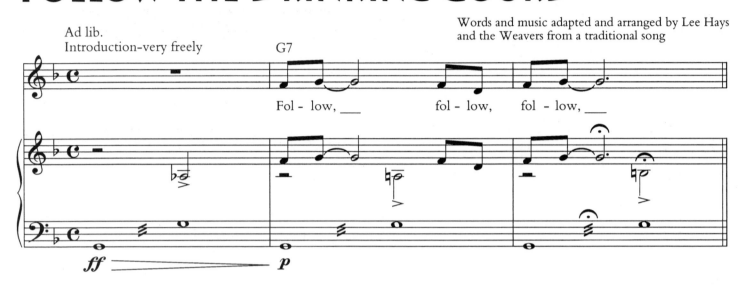

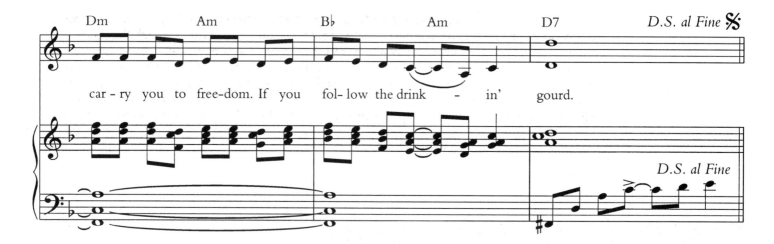

D.S. al Fine 𝄋

car - ry you to free-dom. If you fol- low the drink - in' gourd.

The riverbank will make a very good road,
The dead trees show you the way,
Left foot, peg foot, traveling on—
Follow the drinking gourd.   *Chorus*

The river ends between two hills,
Follow the drinking gourd,
There's another river on the other side,
Follow the drinking gourd.   *Chorus*

Where the great big river meets the little river,
Follow the drinking gourd,
The old man is a-waitin' for to carry you to freedom,
If you follow the drinking gourd.   *Chorus*

As his granddaughter works in the kitchen, a southern woodcutter trades his ax for a brief rest and a cooling cup of water.

On January 1, 1863, President Abraham Lincoln signed the Emancipation Proclamation, which officially released all slaves from bondage in the South. As the word spread through the slave cabins, blacks began to move, slowly at first and then in ever-swelling numbers, away from the plantations and toward the Union armies. John Eaton, a contemporary observer, said the slave population's movement—a people "rising up and leaving its ancient bondage, . . . coming garbed in rags or in silks, with feet shod or bleeding, individually or in families and larger groups"—was like "the oncoming of cities." As they moved toward freedom, the people sang of those who had gone before them and of everything they were jubilantly leaving forever: the call, the lash, and the "peck of corn" and "pint of salt," slavery's rations.

MANY THOUSAND GONE

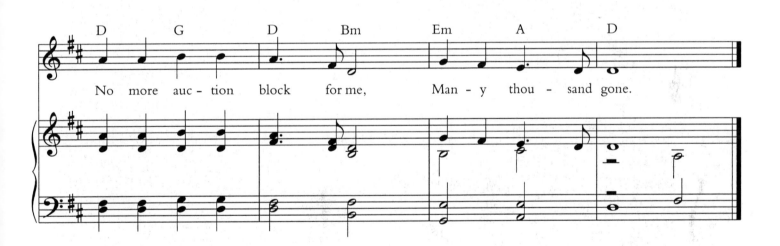

No more peck of corn for me,
No more, no more;
No more peck of corn for me,
Many thousand gone.

No more driver's lash for me. *Chorus*

No more pint o'salt for me. *Chorus*

No more hundred lash for me. *Chorus*

No more mistress' call for me. *Chorus*

Sometimes the deepest feelings can be best expressed by the simplest language. The melody and rhythm are rudimentary, the rhyme is nonexistent, and the author is everyone present: anyone can contribute a line. The end result—a song such as "I Want To Go Home"—is a whole that is far greater than its parts.

"I Want To Go Home" demonstrates a profound desire to reach heaven, where there is no rain, no tribulation, no slavery. This is a theme that recurs constantly in slave music. "This world is not my home/ I'm only passin' through"; "Don't know what my mother wants to stay here fuh/ Dis ole world ain't been no friend to huh"—these are typical lines. Colonel Thomas Higgenson, the white Massachusetts officer who commanded a celebrated black regiment in the Civil War, listened to his men sing one evening:

> *I'll lie in de grave and stretch out my arms,*
> *Lay dis body down.*
> *I go to de judgment in de evenin' of de day,*
> *When I lay dis body down.*

"Never, it seems to me, since man first lived and suffered," wrote Higgenson, "was his infinite longing for peace uttered more plaintively."

I WANT TO GO HOME

Dere's no sun to burn you,
O yes, I want to go home, want to go home.

similarly

Dere's no hard trials . . .

Dere's no whips a-crackin' . . .

Dere's no stormy weather . . .

Dere's no tribulation . . .

No more slavery in de Kingdom . . .

No evil-doers in de Kingdom . . .

All is gladness in de Kingdom . . .

A cart man plies his trade with ox power, a valuable energy source in the almost horseless post– Civil War South.

The concept of the "Valiant Soldier"—an almost-magical being who would help bear the burdens of slavery and eventually lead a strike for freedom—was an enduring one among slaves. This song also illustrates the personal connection that religious slaves felt toward their deity: "O Lord, I want. . ." the petitioner sings confidently. The same themes—intimacy with the Lord, the need for the Valiant Soldier—surface in many songs. Here is another example:

Gwine to argue wid de Father and chatter wid de Son,
The last trumpet call shall sound, I'll be there.
Gwine talk 'bout de bright world dey jes' come from.
The last trumpet shall sound, I'll be there.

Gwine to write to Massa Jesus,
To send some Valiant Soldier
To turn back Pharaoh's army, Hallelu!

SOME VALIANT SOLDIER

cross. For I weep, I weep. I can't hold out. If an-y mer-cy,

Lord, O pit-y poor me. For I me.

Playing his homemade fiddle in 1880, a youngster sits outside the cabin his family has occupied since slavery days.

When emancipation finally came, black men and women all over the South celebrated the glory that overcame them. In Petersburg, Virginia, former slaves danced around a fire, singing this song:

I's free, I's free, I's free at las'!
Thank God A'mighty, I's free at las'!

I fasted an' I prayed till I came thew
Thank God A'mighty, I's free at las'!

Marching through Georgia, a soldier in Sherman's army heard black voices singing:

Shout the glad tidings o'er Egypt's dark sea,
Jehovah has triumphed, his people are free!

And when the North captured Richmond, Virginia, newly freed blacks ran through the streets, shouting "Slavery Chain Done Broke at Last," a joyous hymn set to the tune of the well-known spiritual "Joshua Fit the Battle of Jericho."

SLAVERY CHAIN DONE BROKE AT LAST

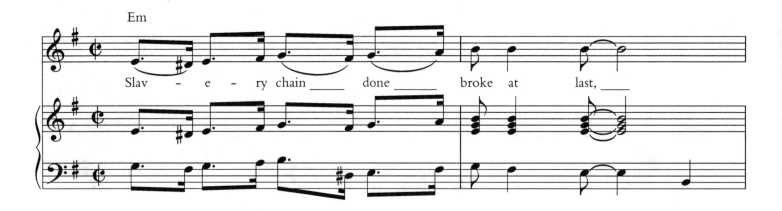

broke at last, ___ Gon - na praise God till I die.

Fine

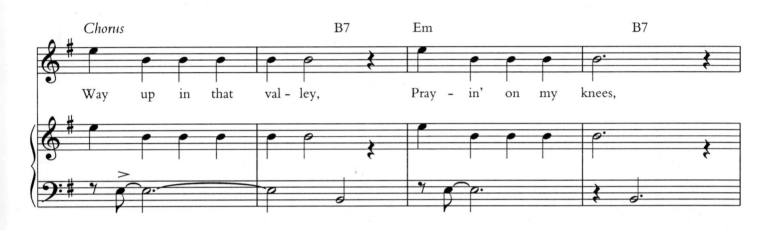

Chorus

Way up in that val - ley, Pray - in' on my knees,

Tell - in' God a - bout my trou- bles, And to help me if He please.

D.C. al Fine

I did tell him how I suffer,
In the dungeon and the chain;
And the days I went with head bowed down,
An' my broken flesh and pain. *Chorus*

I did know my Jesus heard me,
'Cause the spirit spoke to me,
An' said, "Rise my chile, your children
An' you too shall be free." *Chorus*

I done p'int one mighty captain
For to marshall all my hosts;
An' to bring my bleeding ones to me,
An' not one shall be lost. *Chorus*

Now no more weary trav'lin',
'Cause my Jesus set me free,
An' there's no more auction block for me
Since He give me liberty. *Chorus*

Index to Titles

Index to First Lines

Jerry Silverman is one of America's most prolific authors of music books. He has a B.S. degree in music from the City College of New York and an M.A. in musicology from New York University. He has authored some 100 books dealing with various aspects of guitar, banjo, violin, and fiddle technique, as well as numerous songbooks and arrangements for other instruments. He teaches guitar and music to children and adults and performs in folk-song concerts before audiences of all ages.

Kenneth B. Clark received a Ph.D. in social psychology from Columbia University and is the author of numerous books and articles on race and education. His books include *Prejudice and Your Child, Dark Ghetto,* and *Pathos of Power.* Long noted as an authority on segregation in schools, his work was cited by the U.S. Supreme Court in its decision in the historic *Brown v. Board of Education of Topeka* case in 1954. Dr. Clark, Distinguished Professor of Psychology Emeritus at the City University of New York, is the president of Kenneth B. Clark & Associates, a consulting firm specializing in personnel matters, race relations, and affirmative action programs.